# THE STEAMPUNK AUTHOR'S WORKBOOK

## A WORKBOOK TO HELP YOU DEVELOP GREAT STEAMPUNK CHARACTERS, LOCATIONS, PLOT IDEAS AND MORE!

LAURA DE LA CRUZ

# Dedication

For those who love and live steampunk!

# How to use this workbook

Use this workbook to develop your plot ideas, characters and location descriptions!  Meant to be used for multiple books (25 sets of 4 worksheets per book), it offers you the opportunity to develop a character or location and save for future reference!

"Steampunk is...a joyous fantasy of the past, allowing us to revel in a nostalgia for what never was. It is a literary playground for adventure, spectacle, drama, escapism and exploration. But most of all it is fun!"
— George Mann

# PLOT IDEAS

# Plot Ideas

NAME IDEAS:

DESCRIPTION/PERSONALITY:

# Location ideas:

_______________________________
_______________________________
_______________________________
_______________________________
_______________________________
_______________________________

# Other ideas:

_______________________________
_______________________________
_______________________________
_______________________________
_______________________________
_______________________________
_______________________________
_______________________________
_______________________________
_______________________________
_______________________________
_______________________________
_______________________________
_______________________________
_______________________________

# PLOT IDEAS

# Plot Ideas

# Name ideas:

_______________________________________

_______________________________________

_______________________________________

_______________________________________

## Description/Personality:

_______________________________________

_______________________________________

_______________________________________

_______________________________________

_______________________________________

_______________________________________

_______________________________________

_______________________________________

_______________________________________

_______________________________________

_______________________________________

_______________________________________

_______________________________________

_______________________________________

_______________________________________

# Location ideas:

________________________________________
________________________________________
________________________________________
________________________________________
________________________________________
________________________________________
________________________________________

# Other ideas:

________________________________________
________________________________________
________________________________________
________________________________________
________________________________________
________________________________________
________________________________________
________________________________________
________________________________________
________________________________________
________________________________________
________________________________________
________________________________________
________________________________________

# PLOT IDEAS

# PLOT IDEAS

NAME IDEAS:

_______________________________________

_______________________________________

_______________________________________

_______________________________________

DESCRIPTION/PERSONALITY:

_______________________________________

_______________________________________

_______________________________________

_______________________________________

_______________________________________

_______________________________________

_______________________________________

_______________________________________

_______________________________________

_______________________________________

_______________________________________

_______________________________________

_______________________________________

_______________________________________

_______________________________________

## Location ideas:

## Other ideas:

# PLOT IDEAS

# Plot Ideas

# Name ideas:

__________________________

__________________________

__________________________

__________________________

# Description/Personality:

_______________________________

_______________________________

_______________________________

_______________________________

_______________________________

_______________________________

_______________________________

_______________________________

_______________________________

_______________________________

_______________________________

_______________________________

_______________________________

_______________________________

_______________________________

_______________________________

_______________________________

_______________________________

## LOCATION IDEAS:

## OTHER IDEAS:

# PLOT IDEAS

# PLOT IDEAS

NAME IDEAS:

_______________________________________

_______________________________________

_______________________________________

DESCRIPTION/PERSONALITY:

_______________________________________
_______________________________________
_______________________________________
_______________________________________
_______________________________________
_______________________________________
_______________________________________
_______________________________________
_______________________________________
_______________________________________
_______________________________________
_______________________________________
_______________________________________
_______________________________________
_______________________________________

# Location ideas:

# Other ideas:

# Plot Ideas

# PLOT IDEAS

## Name ideas:

_______________________________
_______________________________

_______________________________

_______________________________

### Description/Personality:

_______________________________
_______________________________
_______________________________
_______________________________
_______________________________
_______________________________
_______________________________
_______________________________
_______________________________
_______________________________
_______________________________
_______________________________
_______________________________
_______________________________
_______________________________
_______________________________

# Location ideas:

_______________________________
_______________________________
_______________________________
_______________________________
_______________________________
_______________________________

# Other ideas:

_______________________________
_______________________________
_______________________________
_______________________________
_______________________________
_______________________________
_______________________________
_______________________________
_______________________________
_______________________________
_______________________________
_______________________________
_______________________________
_______________________________

# Plot Ideas

# PLOT IDEAS

# Name ideas:

_______________________________

_______________________________

_______________________________

_______________________________

## Description/Personality:

_______________________________

_______________________________

_______________________________

_______________________________

_______________________________

_______________________________

_______________________________

_______________________________

_______________________________

_______________________________

_______________________________

_______________________________

_______________________________

_______________________________

_______________________________

_______________________________

# Location ideas:

_______________________________
_______________________________
_______________________________
_______________________________
_______________________________
_______________________________

# Other ideas:

_______________________________
_______________________________
_______________________________
_______________________________
_______________________________
_______________________________
_______________________________
_______________________________
_______________________________
_______________________________
_______________________________
_______________________________
_______________________________
_______________________________

# PLOT IDEAS

# PLOT IDEAS

# Name ideas:

_______________________
_______________________
_______________________

## Description/Personality:

_______________________
_______________________
_______________________
_______________________
_______________________
_______________________
_______________________
_______________________
_______________________
_______________________
_______________________
_______________________
_______________________
_______________________
_______________________
_______________________

## Location ideas:

_______________________________________
_______________________________________
_______________________________________
_______________________________________
_______________________________________
_______________________________________

## Other ideas:

_______________________________________
_______________________________________
_______________________________________
_______________________________________
_______________________________________
_______________________________________
_______________________________________
_______________________________________
_______________________________________
_______________________________________
_______________________________________
_______________________________________

# Plot Ideas

# Plot Ideas

# Name ideas:

_______________________

_______________________

_______________________

_______________________

## Description/Personality:

_______________________

_______________________

_______________________

_______________________

_______________________

_______________________

_______________________

_______________________

_______________________

_______________________

_______________________

_______________________

_______________________

_______________________

_______________________

_______________________

_______________________

## Location ideas:

## Other ideas:

# PLOT IDEAS

# PLOT IDEAS

# Name ideas:

_______________________________
_______________________________
_______________________________
_______________________________

# Description/Personality:

_______________________________
_______________________________
_______________________________
_______________________________
_______________________________
_______________________________
_______________________________
_______________________________
_______________________________
_______________________________
_______________________________
_______________________________
_______________________________
_______________________________
_______________________________
_______________________________

# LOCATION IDEAS:

## OTHER IDEAS:

# PLOT IDEAS

# Plot Ideas

# Name ideas:

 

# Description/Personality:

# Location ideas:

_______________________________
_______________________________
_______________________________
_______________________________
_______________________________
_______________________________

# Other ideas:

_______________________________
_______________________________
_______________________________
_______________________________
_______________________________
_______________________________
_______________________________
_______________________________
_______________________________
_______________________________
_______________________________
_______________________________
_______________________________
_______________________________

# PLOT IDEAS

# PLOT IDEAS

## Name ideas:

_______________________________

_______________________________

_______________________________

_______________________________

## Description/Personality:

_______________________________

_______________________________

_______________________________

_______________________________

_______________________________

_______________________________

_______________________________

_______________________________

_______________________________

_______________________________

_______________________________

_______________________________

_______________________________

_______________________________

_______________________________

_______________________________

_______________________________

# Location ideas:

## Other ideas:

# PLOT IDEAS

# PLOT IDEAS

NAME IDEAS:

DESCRIPTION/PERSONALITY:

## Location ideas:

## Other ideas:

# Plot Ideas

# Plot Ideas

## Name ideas:

_______________________

_______________________

_______________________

## Description/Personality:

_______________________

_______________________

_______________________

_______________________

_______________________

_______________________

_______________________

_______________________

_______________________

_______________________

_______________________

_______________________

_______________________

_______________________

_______________________

_______________________

_______________________

# Location ideas:

___________________________________________
___________________________________________
___________________________________________
___________________________________________
___________________________________________
___________________________________________

# Other ideas:

___________________________________________
___________________________________________
___________________________________________
___________________________________________
___________________________________________
___________________________________________
___________________________________________
___________________________________________
___________________________________________
___________________________________________
___________________________________________
___________________________________________
___________________________________________
___________________________________________

# PLOT IDEAS

# Plot Ideas

Name ideas:

_______________________________________

_______________________________________

_______________________________________

_______________________________________

Description/Personality:

## LOCATION IDEAS:

## OTHER IDEAS:

# PLOT IDEAS

# PLOT IDEAS

NAME IDEAS:

DESCRIPTION/PERSONALITY:

# Location ideas:

_______________________________________

_______________________________________

_______________________________________

_______________________________________

_______________________________________

_______________________________________

# Other ideas:

_______________________________________

_______________________________________

_______________________________________

_______________________________________

_______________________________________

_______________________________________

_______________________________________

_______________________________________

_______________________________________

_______________________________________

_______________________________________

_______________________________________

_______________________________________

# PLOT IDEAS

# PLOT IDEAS

# Name ideas:

_______________________________

_______________________________

_______________________________

_______________________________

# Description/Personality:

_______________________________

_______________________________

_______________________________

_______________________________

_______________________________

_______________________________

_______________________________

_______________________________

_______________________________

_______________________________

_______________________________

_______________________________

_______________________________

_______________________________

_______________________________

_______________________________

# Location ideas:

# Other ideas:

# Plot Ideas

# Plot Ideas

NAME IDEAS:

DESCRIPTION/PERSONALITY:

# Location ideas:

# Other ideas:

# Plot Ideas

# Plot Ideas

# Name ideas:

# Description/Personality:

# LOCATION IDEAS:

# OTHER IDEAS:

# Plot Ideas

# Plot Ideas

# Name ideas:

_______________________________________

_______________________________________

_______________________________________

## Description/Personality:

_______________________________________

_______________________________________

_______________________________________

_______________________________________

_______________________________________

_______________________________________

_______________________________________

_______________________________________

_______________________________________

_______________________________________

_______________________________________

_______________________________________

_______________________________________

_______________________________________

_______________________________________

_______________________________________

## LOCATION IDEAS:

________________________________________
________________________________________
________________________________________
________________________________________
________________________________________
________________________________________

## OTHER IDEAS:

________________________________________
________________________________________
________________________________________
________________________________________
________________________________________
________________________________________
________________________________________
________________________________________
________________________________________
________________________________________
________________________________________
________________________________________
________________________________________

# PLOT IDEAS

# Plot Ideas

NAME IDEAS:

DESCRIPTION/PERSONALITY:

# LOCATION IDEAS:

# OTHER IDEAS:

# Plot Ideas

# PLOT IDEAS

NAME IDEAS:

DESCRIPTION/PERSONALITY:

# Location ideas:

# Other ideas:

# PLOT IDEAS

# PLOT IDEAS

# Name ideas:

_______________________________
_______________________________
_______________________________
_______________________________

## Description/Personality:

_______________________________
_______________________________
_______________________________
_______________________________
_______________________________
_______________________________
_______________________________
_______________________________
_______________________________
_______________________________
_______________________________
_______________________________
_______________________________
_______________________________
_______________________________
_______________________________
_______________________________

# Location ideas:

_______________________________________________
_______________________________________________
_______________________________________________
_______________________________________________
_______________________________________________
_______________________________________________

# Other ideas:

_______________________________________________
_______________________________________________
_______________________________________________
_______________________________________________
_______________________________________________
_______________________________________________
_______________________________________________
_______________________________________________
_______________________________________________
_______________________________________________
_______________________________________________
_______________________________________________
_______________________________________________
_______________________________________________

# Plot Ideas

# PLOT IDEAS

Name ideas:

_______________________________
_______________________________
_______________________________

Description/Personality:
_______________________________
_______________________________
_______________________________
_______________________________
_______________________________
_______________________________
_______________________________
_______________________________
_______________________________
_______________________________
_______________________________
_______________________________
_______________________________
_______________________________
_______________________________
_______________________________
_______________________________

# Location ideas:

________________________________________
________________________________________
________________________________________
________________________________________
________________________________________
________________________________________

# Other ideas:

________________________________________
________________________________________
________________________________________
________________________________________
________________________________________
________________________________________
________________________________________
________________________________________
________________________________________
________________________________________
________________________________________
________________________________________
________________________________________
________________________________________

# Plot Ideas

# PLOT IDEAS

# Name ideas:

_________________________________________

_________________________________________

_________________________________________

_________________________________________

## Description/Personality:

_________________________________________

_________________________________________

_________________________________________

_________________________________________

_________________________________________

_________________________________________

_________________________________________

_________________________________________

_________________________________________

_________________________________________

_________________________________________

_________________________________________

_________________________________________

_________________________________________

_________________________________________

_________________________________________

_________________________________________

_________________________________________

# Location ideas:

# Other ideas:

# THANK YOU FOR BUYING THIS BOOK!

I hope you enjoyed this workbook and found some value in it.  Thank you, thank you!


"Indeed. I have often thought that when a man selects one word over another he often reveals far more of himself than he intended."

- Mark Hodder, The Strange Affair of Spring Heeled Jack

www.ingramcontent.com/pod-product-compliance
Lightning Source LLC
Chambersburg PA
CBHW050929260726
48660CB00001B/473